MW01617178

Pocket
Full of
Love

Written by Lisa Pepper-Satkin, MFT

Illustrated by Andrea Longar

Copyright © 2018 by Lisa Pepper-Satkin.

All rights reserved. No part of this publication may be reproduced, distributed or transmitted in any form or by any means, including photocopying, recording, or other electronic or mechanical methods, without the prior written permission of the publisher, except in the case of brief quotations embodied in critical reviews and certain other noncommercial uses permitted by copyright law. For permission requests, write to the publisher, addressed "Attention: Permissions Coordinator," at the address below.

Pepper & Pop Publishing
1774 Union Street
San Francisco, CA 94123
pepperandpoppublishing.com
lisa@lisapeppersatkin.com
Phone: 415-225-6925

Illustrated by Andrea Longar

Ordering Information:
Quantity sales. Special discounts are available on quantity purchases by corporations, associations, and others. For details, contact the "Special Sales Department" at the address above.

Pocket Full of Love/ Lisa Pepper-Satkin, MFT.—1st ed.
ISBN 978-0-9987676-0-4 paperback
ISBN 978-0-9987676-1-1 hardback
ISBN 978-0-9987676-2-8 ebook
Library of Congress Control Number: 2018957104

DEDICATION

I lovingly dedicate this to every child who suffers because of their fear and anxiety. And to Audrey with the biggest LOVE you can imagine. Your dedication to taming your anxiety has motivated me to keep going. Your poppies are on these pages. Thank you from the bottom of my heart. And to every single person who has ever told me they believe that my work with children matters. It matters more than anyone of us will ever know.

Ella was a kind, sweet girl. She loved animals and magical stories. She loved to wear polka-dots and stripes together. Ice cream, pizza, and popcorn were her favorite foods.

There was one thing, though, which Ella did not love. Sometimes she felt very afraid, way down deep, right inside the center of her heart. Even though she tried really hard, she couldn't make her fearful thoughts go away.

She noticed that she was scared to raise her hand in class.

She was afraid to talk to new friends.

She was even afraid to ask for what she really wanted or needed.

She imagined that none of her friends ever felt the same way.

Ella felt confused when she heard people say, "She's so shy." She knew she wasn't shy! Ella's fear made her thoughts foggy. She often felt lost inside of her thinking, and this made her seem shy.

Ella wondered what it would be like to feel less afraid.

On her way home from school one day, Ella experienced the most amazing and magical thing: She started seeing hearts everywhere! She saw hearts in nature, hearts on sidewalks, and hearts in flowers! Ella even found hearts in the water drops on the sidewalk.

Ella imagined that with every heart she spotted, her fearful thinking got smaller. She noticed how safe she felt with all of the hearts around. The more she focused on hearts and love, the less afraid she felt. She called this feeling "BIGlove."

That night in her dreams, Ella took a huge sewing needle and stitched together all the hearts she saw in the world with a long, red ribbon. The hearts each had a pocket with a safe place for writing or drawing pictures about her worries and fears. She saw the ribbon connecting the hearts of people everywhere. She knew this would make life so much sweeter.

Ella woke up excited and shared her dream with her mom. She told her mom she wanted to do something to help the world and share more LOVE. She said, "I have a great way to do this. We will make a toy that will send BIGlove to everyone."

The toy Ella had in mind had a BIG heart-shaped head and a red ribbon holding the pocket. She couldn't wait to make one with her mom. She named it HeartyKid. It was very bright, colorful, and had that small pocket around the neck where she could put secret notes.

In the notes, she reminded herself that when she felt afraid and her thinking was foggy, "Lean on love instead of worry or fear," she wrote. She put the note in her new HeartyKid's pocket. She was determined to practice being brave.

The next day, Mrs. Drake called on her in class. Ella felt the fear bubble deep inside her heart. She imagined a little voice saying, "No, don't do it, this could be scary." She knew this was her crooked thinking. She remembered her HeartyKid, her note about being brave, and all the love she had found.

She shot her hand high into the air. She told herself "I am safe" and, "I am brave!" She imagined the bright red ribbon connecting her with everyone in the classroom.

When she was called on, she boldly answered Mrs. Drake's question. She quieted her fear and moved through her day with a new calm.

Ella ran home and shared this story with her mom. Her mom said, "What you feel at times – that crooked thinking – is called anxiety. It's a normal thing, but feeling it too much can be painful. Your idea to spread HeartyKid love and compassion is fantastic, and could provide comfort when other kids feel anxious."

Ella kept her HeartyKid near her. Whenever she felt stuck in her feelings, she tucked a note about her fear in the special pocket. Even though she stuck many notes in the pocket, there was always room for more. The best part was that the more she worked with her worries, the smaller they became.

That weekend, Ella and her mom started making HeartyKid toys. With each one they made, Ella set off to spread love. She felt more joy than ever before. She couldn't resist making just one more toy. She wanted everyone to have a HeartyKid to help them overcome their fears.

She told her mom, "I'm showing fear who is boss!" At that moment, she decided to focus on finding connection to as many hearts as she could and spreading love with her HeartyKid.

And now she has reached YOU!

Who can YOU share HeartyKid love with?

the End

Please remember to use the groovy pocket around my HeartyKid's neck! That special place is to remind you just how BRAVE, BOLD & SMART you are.

Here are things YOU can do with your HeartyKid toy:

-Write notes of LOVE and compassion (which can heal others) and put them in the pocket.

-Put ideas in the pocket of your toy and watch your focus grow.

-Write examples of how you are BRAVE, BOLD & SMART (email us at info@myHeartyKid.com) and we will send you a FREE sticker!

-Heal your own heart/fears by reminding yourself that your own HeartyKid connects you to the Universal Heart - a BIG force of LOVE.

Lisa ♡ ♡

Lisa Pepper-Satkin, MFT is a Licensed Psychotherapist and an Executive Therapeutic Coach www.lisapeppersatkin.com and has been in practice for over 25 years. She has a Master's Degree in Psychology. Her fierce love of creativity and connecting people to their deepest truth drives her successful work. Lisa also created myHeartyKid, a fabulous program which teaches kids how to have fun with Social Emotional Learning. She commits her free time to volunteering in classrooms teaching kids and teachers about SELF (Social Emotional Learning made FUN). www.myHeartyKid.com. She happily provides myHeartyKid free for educators. She is married and raising two daughters in California.

Andrea 🌸

Andrea Longar is a creative woman with an incalculable passion for art. Fashion designer by profession and artist at heart. She has worked in the fashion industry in denim and children's textile design, and in the arts as a muralist and illustrator. She is currently a children's illustrator and textile prints designer.

Dear Reader!

I hope you and your kids enjoyed this book as much as I enjoyed writing it. If you did, it would be wonderful if you would take a short minute to leave a review online wherever you found this book. Your kind feedback is super important and much appreciated.

You can also write to me at lisa@lisapeppersatkin.com or info@myheartykid.com.

Gratefully,

Lisa Pepper-Satkin

Pepper & Pop Publishing

"This is ____'s Book"

27251604R00022

Made in the USA
Columbia, SC
09 October 2018